# BURIED CHOIRS

# Buried Choirs

Katharine Rauk

**TINDERBOX
EDITIONS**

Tinderbox Editions
Molly Sutton Kiefer, Publisher and Editor
Red Wing, Minnesota
tinderboxeditions@gmail.com
www.tinderboxeditions.org


Cover design by Nikkita Cohoon
Cover art by Fred Michel, "Papaver somniferum" (2012, digital photograph)
Interior design by Nikkita Cohoon
Author photo by William Cameron

# Contents

# BURIED CHOIRS

# A PREAMBLE TO AN EXPLANATION OF YOU

It was like I worked in a Popsicle factory
but had never tasted the color red.
I walked the dry tongue of the road
as crickets *scritch scritch scitched*
little tin ladders up from the ditches at night
but never once did I climb them to the moon.
Which was just another stone to kick,
and I was a graveyard shift without the machinery
of the stars. My heart was a vacant elevator
opening and shutting uselessly on each floor,
it couldn't make a dime panhandling under a bridge,
I was January's sedan without all four doors.
Doubt rode me bareback across the edge of small towns
while postage stamps in my pocket cried out
to be kissed. The conveyer belts of the ocean
never carried me away. I never swam through clouds
of krill. I did not buy clementines
just to see that fine mist spray when I broke open
their skins, did not have it coat my fingers and palms
as if I had crawled many miles through dust fine as powdered sugar
on my hands and knees. I wasn't dust.
I wasn't the scent of dust kicked up by horses' hooves.
I wasn't the voice of dust held in the Sahara's mouth.
I wasn't even the caress of dust
as it lingered over footprints you might have once made.

# THE GREATEST SHOW

I am collecting quarters in an old cigar box.
The lid has a picture of a mermaid perched
on a rock. Waves crack like wineglasses
all around her, and the color of her tail
matches the color of my mother's eyes when
she listens to too much Liszt after dinner.
But nothing adds up to the weight of that coin
I am always hiding beneath my tongue.

Step right up, little dreamer! Even the sea
is just a ship / is just a dress / is just a night
is going for broke towards every shore—

# AN OPEN LETTER TO MY IMAGINARY FRIEND

I have written a song
in which I am just one bar
of soap upon which water
can play its innumerable
fingers. I grow
smaller and smaller until
I cease to exist

except in your head,
which is what I invented
it to do. In there
I can say *that white cloud*
and be understood
because of the field
of language where I mean

to lie down with you.
Though the wind blows
the clover away, I'm good
at keeping things
quiet. Here, take it,
this chain of sunlight
I've woven for our hair.

# CLOGGED ONLY WITH MUSIC LIKE THE WHEELS OF BIRDS

There's no such thing as a white dress.
Shadows pocket in tucked-up hemlines

and eyeholes of buttons or lace. In folds
of pleats and shifts. So I'll give you the slip

if you try to pin my heart
upon my sleeve. I'm like the figment moon

(a fragrance of your imagination)
and my mouth is a seam

because I never tell. I am queen
of seeming. When I said my unmentionables

are impenetrable, I only meant
sometimes. Here is my red

pincushion, most holy of holies.
Here's the needle used to pierce

my sweetmeats for the string. Meanwhile,
me and my white dress

are upstairs being blue—unrolling reams of sky
for wind to roam, being blown

in our own good time and room.

# INSTRUCTIONS ON HOW TO PLAY THE COMB

If you practice, you might make it as big as Mrs. Delilah's hair those mornings she no longer had to get her son to the bus stop but could fill the extra hour in an empty house teasing herself into oblivion.

Take a comb. Fold a piece of cigarette paper over it. Blow.

When Mrs. Delilah stood in front of the pull-down Map of the World, she was not anything you could moor a boat to. Nobody cried *Rapunzel!* from the small island of light her bedroom window cast upon the grass.

Listen. It's not true that the hair of the dead continues to grow.

No one could tell what Mrs. Delilah was thinking as she shuffled our papers, but "Grass is the beautiful uncut hair of graves" is what she said.

Hum into the teeth of the comb. Who's that standing in the doorway with brambled hems, the scent of wildroot oil?

# NOBODY

builds wheels out of salt
as this is the same as inviting a stranger
into bed when you are burning
with loneliness. Because the roads
are in love with rain and leave
themselves like silk stockings
all over the city. Because you can
slice open a dogwood bud and little storms
spill out like bells chiming every hour on the hour
before dissolving into the wind. Because
marking time is not difficult mathematics
but one you should learn how to sing.
Because you want, whether you know it,
to be ground into grey gears of sea
below gulls that are wheeling
wheeling over those cliffs of salt
that are a body undone in dark or in rain.

# SELF-ASSESSMENT

I am trying to orchestrate a performance
report for the Dean, though he'll read it off a screen
when all I ever wanted was to see my name
in print. I'll just be a projection
of his distance: not the jet planes flying in formation
but the photographic reproduction of said
formation that's pinned to the corkboard in his corner
office. According to the Law of Accelerating
Returns (at least the version I discovered
my student cut and pasted from the web
and is the only version I know) it won't be long
before robots designed like red blood cells
will sail down my arteries to deliver
micropillows of air. Goodbye being
winded. Goodbye gulps and gasps and
breeze through the double windows
of my lungs. Wasn't much to see: a blank
sky, a border of illegible footnotes
my toes once sang in the grass.

# ROUGH DRAFT WORKSHOP

We did the best we could
but Musu couldn't tell the difference

between past and present
tense, so we were all confused.

Was the gunfire happening now
or had it happened last night

in her nightmares again?
There was no conclusion

to Jasmin's essay.
We did the best we could,

but she was hearing a voice
and wasn't sure if it was her Father

or the devil, so she was put on
medication. It was impossible

to discuss transitions
between paragraphs when Erika

was sick with the two babies,
Mai was sick with the baby

she had lost, and Kelly's boyfriend
told her she was first-rate at fucking

up. So we outlined and revised
and erased, which was the best

of all we thought we could do.

# HAVE TORN OFF THE WHOLE OF MAY

and June, plus a measure of July.
If only days could fit in pockets

as easily as I carry night inside

my head. Sometimes I cry out
in the dumb dark—There is nothing

more holy than love! Too bad

that's not something I can feel
on my tongue. It is tempting

now and again to go black-

berrying, a girl who drowned
herself wrote in a letter.

As if even a small body

of water wasn't sweet enough,
might have been refused.

# ENORMOUS DREAM GUMBALL MACHINE

Stick a quarter in the slot,
or a nickel, or a knife.
Whatever you've got:
some kids, some books,
your own good name
that's worth shit, really.
But it's best not to think
too hard about what it is
you want. Some candy
keeps its own cosmos—
like eyeballs of the dead
that refuse to give up
their final vision—Orange
and terrible, or otherwise.

# THE UNIVERSE

Two nutmegs may be struck together
to make sparks. You can burn down
a whole cabinet factory this way!
That's why I like to read recipes
or old phone books left on the curb.
Dear Fanny Kowalski or Carl Ruiz,
I am often lonely and imagine the rain
falling on no one as it is wont to do
at sea. Then I become a little less
lonely, but more musical. To compose
oneself in the face of whatever
emptiness sings into the loosening
currents is to be alive. Is to let
wind pluck the cables that bridge
the distance between each rock-ribbed
shore. Is to hold you here in my kitchen,
a window smashed with light.

# RITUAL

I set a corncake at the edge
of the woods and

wait because I heard
that's where you go
to make friends. The night

is no machine. When I poke it
with a stick, the jelly spurts out

like a promise I imagine
you gave. Tastes like
some made-up ramble in the rain

which is my favorite kind
of torture: it's too cold

but I'm happy because your hair
makes spokes for the wheeling
universe that holds us

in place where we are
shaking loose, and as far as I am

concerned (because later
I'll take the bus uptown
and the sun will come out)

those are the only crumbs
I really need.

# THE PRICE

Something I can't bear is that I think
I will never learn what love is

eating out of your hand: cracked
corn, maybe millet, black oil

sunflower seed. The glossy shell
is what I think of when

I am not thinking of you
thinking of yesterday and the price

of tulips in Kalamazoo
or other people's eyes or

whatever it is you think of
when you're not thinking of me

as I really am: a calendar
full of all the Thursdays that were

and will ever be: like doorframes
stacked one up against

another's emptiness: and then some
kind of wind blowing through.

# MY GOD

is a gorgeous Greek statue
with his dick broke off.
I built him that way:
I like to lack
as it always gets me
to lick the tip
of my metaphorical pencil
to point myself in all the directions
but here. Like at his crotch,
which is a vacancy
sign at some roadside motel
where I check myself in
on nights the moon
is an icy highball
sailing me into the sound
the semis make going down on
Hwy 53, as good as
anything for forgetting
the past. Such as the time
I was gathering cloud-
berries (yes, cloudberries
are a real thing that I didn't make
up) and My God
appeared beside me in the wet
meadow, all Zamboni marble
and glossy slips
of hair. I felt almost
unbruisable and therefore un-
berrylike, but all I could get him to say
was whatever
a shirt whispers over my breasts
when I take it off.

# HORN SOLO ON THE BANKS OF THE RIVER STYX

There are no words
that can hitch

hike up the lone high
way of song to hot

wire the corpse
of everything you left

to joyride broke
cornfields beneath

a carousel sky.
Horse, horse, riderless

horse I can't get in line
or verse even though

there's turning!
Can I rip the mouth

piece out of a sax
O phone to call the other

side of the river: *yoo
hoo, hey you who*

*are almost not
quite here?*

# CAIRN

You needed me
before you needed me

no more. I left
coins and stones

to darken stoops
all over the city

we used to inhabit,
fingers pointing

towards that gash
in the sky even birds

will not traffic.
I hate that I can't help

but cast about for
your eyes that I know

better than to fall into
as if into a meadow

—the bewildered
way the grasses

sway, such
forgeries of light.

# ALL THAT YOU HAVE

The book lies

open on your lap
like the score

of some music you
did not compose.

You: one. The song:
all that you have

not been spared.

# WAITING AT THE EDGE OF THE RIVER AGAIN

When I saw the elk

would not arrive, no matter
how long I waited,

I renounced my faith

in dusk. Not that it wasn't
happening, but that it was

a hunger I chose—

one I knew all along
contained too much

expectation. This was a flash-

light dropped in the scrub.
But damn if I didn't get

down on my knees

to scrabble for it
among night's fluid herds.

# DEAR PROFESSOR

You know how I am
always trying to study

the sun (how it cracks
through the water

glass you are
lifting to your lips

like shards of August,
maybe laughter).

Your lips!
That have eaten

so many dusks!
It's a sickness

we share and
I wouldn't have it

any other way.
In fact, it is precisely

how we know some-
where someone is

constructing a cathedral
out of a box

of macaroni, glue, and
a thousand matchsticks

of light. I am such
a stupid cinder, trying to

fan myself into flame.
Help me become a wind

instrument—a bassoon,
a robin, the sea and

the sea and the sea, poppies
with *faenas* unfolding

in the black
bullrings of their eyes.

Tell me how that sounds.
How blood is cleaned

off the sand after all
the crowds have gone away.

# VALENTINE

You burn like spires of white
pine. Goodbye to the forest

I planted to keep you
away! You are hell-

bent on giving me what I say
I don't want, since

you know my mind
is rarely made up for good.

Love, for all your ravishments
you deserve to eat a cake

of soap. I'm just its bubble.
Please pray for my crash

course in Small Engine Repair
as I'm failing so far

that I'll soon be scraping
the sputtering blades of my heart's

propellers along the wrong
fill-in-the-blank.

# SONATA IN SOMETHING SHARP

I am a little allot-

ment in a survey
of silence. Though

there are no instruments

to track what I will
not ask for—something

I want, or worse,

need—you
are expected to hear.

I hold the key

in which Saturn sings
her moons around

orbits whose inclination

is tiny but
distinguishable never-

theless from zero.

# PARROTOLOGY

Insert a cracked nut, turn
the crank to creak out
your fortune. This bird
spits out a tune you have
heard before, a receipt
like a long white ribbon
for your neck that reads:
*You, sailor on leave,
let's go.* So you go and
are unclocked as a cloud
shipwrecking its own
soundless district—only
the parrot is perched on
your shoulder scratching
its lecture in your ear.
Haven't we all been that
pursuer, also that tireless
immigrant on the winds?

# JEOPARDY

Once a woman in the zero
gravity of a vacuum chamber
fell into unconsciousness as if into a bed
of asters assembled from a flash-
back of stars—and the last thing
she heard before blackout was the hiss
of saliva boiling on her tongue.
Turns out birds need gravity
to swallow, so they couldn't survive in space
even if they had the right kind of wings
to arrive. I'm starting to believe
in angels outside my window.
They sound like clumsy kids knocking
their front teeth together in prelude
to sex, that little snare
drum among the unstoppable symphony
that is the opposite of a closet,
in other words what is sky.

# INSTRUCTIONS ON HOW TO OPEN
A GIFT THAT MAY OR MAY NOT BE
A SAUSAGE

First, please consider the mustard seed, which everyone knows makes an excellent condiment for sausage. As Jesus said in his Sermon on the Meat, the Kingdom of Heaven is like a tiny mustard seed among the fields which will grow into a tree so large that flying pigs may lodge in its branches. But, as the scholars point out, the mustard plant is actually a weed, a subversive gift that is difficult to ungive. Like the gift of love, which once opened cannot be returned to its original package, no matter what your ex-husband says. Yes, I am talking for better or for wurst and all that. Did you know the word *wurst* comes from the Latin *vertere*, or *to turn*? A sausage, once eaten, becomes part of your body, years later curling out from the very roots of your hair. He liked yours windblown, or at least that's what he said. A sausage is the size of a you-know-what, but a mustard seed is the size of what you know.

# CONGRATULATIONS! WE ARE PLEASED

to offer you this black crayon
with which to color your private art collection
of the cosmos. We know how much you love

tangerines. This will take guesswork
out of your hands—such as where and when
to place them on the page

of another person's skin. The answer is
live in service of rapture!—that unrepeatable
playlist of the sea. It knows how to crash

a party, shine its headlights
through the cement-block windows of your brain
where all the depressed poems are

passed out drunk on the floor. Hear those toads
scribbling endless loops of lust
into the congealing darkness behind the mall?

We're quite certain you'll never be one
hundred percent satisfied, but we guarantee
that hue sounds most sublime.

# CHOREOGRAPHY OF ONE WINTER

A vegetable ivory button
on a shirt from some Salvation
Army is what I am
when I want you
to worry me
with your fingers
because it's cold here
and all constellations
are nailed to the sky.
Have you tasted
salt from Antofogasta
where the sea is buried
alive? Have you opened
a window bolted
against small tickets
of snow? Have you felt
the hand of the clock
like a slap of ash
on your face? I have
studied the long division
spilling in chalk
down a blackboard that ends
with a remainder
of one—a white
stroke against the dark
separating the after
from the before.

# DOWSING

When Marco asked his mother what the crab would do without legs, the silence slowly rose about his chest and lapped at the corners of the butter dish. His mother looked away. From then on, Marco's heart was just a dishrag that only got washed on days the windows broadcast sunscapes on the floor. He sniffed bars of pine tar soap and imagined barrel staves pressed up against each other in the dark holds of ships. He arranged and rearranged his shoes. When he opened his mouth, out came a bubble that burst into dangerous glitters of music in the grass. That's why he liked to visit shop windows crowded with mannequins after-hours or the hush of empty pews. He said aloud "Drinking on West Lake as It Clears Then Rains" and "Encountering Dusk on Grave-Sweeping Day with Rich Men and Their Singsong Girls," plus other Chinese poems. The footnote said the first two slashes that establish the pictogram for *beautiful* look like the ears of a divining rod, and Marco traced them again and again.

# TO A TRAVELER

Where are you

walking without me,
are there birds

that reel and stall?

What foyer, what
dusk, what field

is gathering hours

even as I have not
been standing there?

I wish I could change

the color of the sky,
but what dark there is is

irreducible, as I am

no longer the only
strain of weather in the air.

# TRANSMISSION

George had an orgasm every time
he saw, or even thought about,
a safety pin. His wife overlooked
this idiosyncrasy because she found it saved her
a lot of trouble, and even when the seizures began
to lock George in their terrible embrace
so he thrashed about the couch like a rainbow trout
baptized by air, she remained unmoved.
But when George reported he'd received
word—as clear as the sheen on Gabriel's horn, as sure
as the microwave's beam mystically pierces the deepest
recesses of a bean burrito, as sharp as
the command to love thy neighbor
as thyself—his wife decreed enough.
The doctors informed George of the tumor
penetrating his temporal lobe, which he needed
immediately removed. After that he would pass
his wife's sewing basket without a thrill,
or cruise the third aisle of Rite Aid over lunch
without even an itch of titillation,
and lie across the bed from his wife—
the length of his thin body quivering
in darkness—desperate to divine the static
emitting from the satellite dish of her face.

# HALLUCINATION

My friend said we are all just jizz
from God's space junk.

He was sitting on the end of my bed
balling up slices of Wonderbread,
then flicking them into the dirt.

He meant the birds
to eat them, deliver the body
of grain back unto itself.

I think you will want to know how
come there was dirt in my bedroom.

My friend unfolded his grey wings.
He's been dead three years now.
He loved me very much.

## NOTES JOTTED DOWN ON PAPER, THEN CRUMPLED UP

I am leaving
myself in the clouds

for I'm committed

to becoming rain,
something else without

a shape. But still cast

upon the scales
of your voice. As if a song

is something light

cannot pass through
or change.

# NIGHT MUSIC

Crickets tend to congregate in barbershops
because it is where time is keenly counted.
Dark curl. Dark curl. Dark snip on the floor.
They do not drink from that puddle the moon
makes but fold themselves up like umbrellas,
always put away their sewing after prayers.
But every evening the little girl who burns
cinnamon sticks in the doorway will sing
*Bless this city of bells and bridges, bless
the twenty-seven bones in the hand* while
she sweeps the sidewalk, sweeps under all
the chairs. Listen! Music is segmentable
(a chorus)     (a season)     (an insect)
not like the soundless rivers of your hair.

# SUMMER ROMANCE

What the heart wants
is not so much

what it sees
as what it invents:

the ease with which
a field of sun-

flowers will turn
in unison to sip

the light. No less
beautiful for not being

true is the story
we tell ourselves

over and over
again about death.

How it could be
the beginning of

a new season you
wade into waist high,

that floats you
in its golden updraft.

How it probably is
some blossom-

head riddled
with holes the wind left

when it scattered seeds
that now look slant-

wise in the dirt.

# DETERMINATION

I know the wind
is something I feel
but can't touch

like all my dead
grandma's memories
twisted into the fuse-

box of my DNA.
They're the reason
for my habit of cracking

pencils, my love
of orange Chevrolets.
Why there are storms

joyriding through
all the prairie towns
that make up my mind's

indecision. Who am I
going to become?
Sometimes we are given

lightning. Sometimes
the quiet heat
of a padlocked barn.

≈

# THE CLEARING

Stars, by day, hide
like seeds' buried choirs.

At first I loved you
this way. Once I called

a herd of deer floating
through dusk *Vespers*

and was not mistaken.
That was a door

I passed through. I had to
grow out of the dead

of winter: how else
was I to sing?

# DUET

*a duel for four hands*

You are not the AM
frequency of moon

shushing like a steam iron

over that ragged black
fenceline of crows.

You are not the flat

light of November
or the hesitation mid-

bridge of feet, shuffle-soft

as a book of feathers
opening over a river.

You are not the chapter

that ends in a language
of smoke, a kingdom

secondhand to a fire.

You are not the burn
of ice against a tongue.

You are the hinge

between hours, a hairpin
turn on a road

after which time begins

to sail backwards.
You are the dark

rain troubling the blossoms

and their spring vow
of white, the abbreviations

of lovers knifed

in the bark of a tree.
You are the argument

between sea and wind,

how one breaks
the other against the rocks,

how two bodies can sing.

# CORONAL MASS EJECTION

Wish I could blame the solar storm
that blitzed the earth with electromagnetic rays,
rerouted several commercial airlines,
and caused all the geese to fly west,
the compass needles in their heads
playing spin the bottle over a rowdy Pacific.
Satellite communications were disrupted,
electric eels in Peru forgot how to sing,
and all the iPhones in the world blinked black—
so for a few seconds everyone looked up to see
moths shivering the air like tiny chandeliers.
Truth is your glance shortcuts every traffic light
in my heart so now no one's in charge,
I'm accelerating down the expressway
of a tuba's gold dream. With one outburst
from your hair, I sputter like a firefly drowning
in champagne. Just imagining the charged particles
of your lips colliding with mine
and I'm watching the northern lights, those bodies
flaring across winter sheets of sky.

# THE QUICKENING

*at twenty weeks pregnant*

One morning at the beach, a girl tipped
a bucket of fish in my lap

and I was rudely hauled up
out of myself, left reeling in the shock of cold slick

bodies on my bare skin, their eerie
iridescence drowning out the heat, in the slipperiness

between our worlds,
in the scales laid out like tiles on a roof

and which, in another life,
might have unfurled as feathers on a wing.

# A BRIEF ODE TO EXCESS

My husband buys jumbo jars of olives
at the supercenter grocery club I refuse to enter
due to its devotion to commodity consumption
as regime. But once he gets fully absorbed
in scraping leaves out of the gutters
or rejiggering the Ethernet cord, I crack open
the refrigerator door to slip my fingers into that brine
of greeny sadness I love to savor. Oil dark as mirrors.
Rain smearing into the sea. All the bobbing
olives and their upturned mouths. Come in
to the kitchen, dear! We'll swim out so far
that not even Death, with his seal pelt coat, may touch us.

# JUGS

How they fill and swell
and brim from tops
of shirts. How they joggle

men. For who wouldn't want
the power to pour forth
in more than just a single

milky spurt? How they sugar
the breath and can wet pink
gums. How they mean home

and the warm hum of sleep.
How in their rise and set
they double one

back to that first vessel's rocking
before the waters broke
so that eyes could be opened,

tongue could be loosened,
and thirst—that boundless cup—
could be spilled.

# BEAUTIFUL PATHOLOGY

A redbud tree in spring is basically a fever
erupting on a branch. Oh! The acceleration
with which my heart does proceed
wrote a poet probably
on a jankety sidewalk somewhere in the deep
South. I walk around dizzy with heat
from the shirt of a man I have barely
touched. Because I am always wanting
what the loons want, the trapezists in their throats blazing
in sequins towards another set of hands or else
the concrete. My friend is a composer,
but he can't title his own song.
Sounds like a plum, I told him. Or a sad man
at a cutting board. Please look at my testes statement
my student emailed me instead of thesis statement,
but I think he meant I am afraid
my life has no main point. Like how I am always
trying to construct a sentence out of erasers and Scotch
tape. How I always end up somewhere where words
skitter into the crack between the elevator
and the 89th floor, or like sperm left to evaporate on the sheets
of some sorry motel. Our love of dancing, poetry, and jazz
is due to the metabolic rhythms we inherited
from our jellyfish forbearers, claims at least one zoologist,
which explains how we are all flagellates at heart.

# CASIDA OF THE WEEPING

*for my daughter at one month, after Lorca*

I listen as weeping spills from the roof
of your mouth, and swing, with you in my arms,
through every room of the house
singing. This is what it's like
to be soaked in milk. This is what it's like to want
to run out into the rain with both hands
empty. I'm done being full
like a suitcase stuffed with a river
and all its swarms of golden trout.
But the rain couldn't care less
because each second 4.4 mothers are born
while all over America radiators clang in the night
and caramel Frappuccinos are whipped into a frenzy
and 18-wheelers sail down the interstate past Tallahassee
where someone's painted the mailboxes black.
Somewhere in the heartland there are warehouses stacked with
        paper towels
and clouds stocked with puddles
and a gardener waiting for Our Lady of Immaculate Cauliflower
to step across the mud on tiny, miraculous feet.
There's just so much to ask for: may you please
be joyful, may you taste the nip of sweetness inside a clover bud,
may you cross over the cobblestones that line Damascus Gate,
may you have a child that won't sleep
but that looks up from your breast with Gollum eyes at 3 am,
may your nipples spring leaks
and point like missiles aimed the wrong direction,
may you have as many warring tribes as Afghanistan

and fall in love and feel like an accordion
squeezed between ham-hock hands,
may you reel, may you cast a silver lure,
may you sketch the architecture of the heart a thousand times,
documenting the erasures in ink.
My greedy rosebud, my endless mouth, my immense
violin: sometimes I think I cannot love you
enough. Sometimes I want to leave you on the steps in a basket
    woven from reeds
and wait for the Nile of your flooded eyes to carry you away.
Then I could be rocked by the waters of the bath
or fuck a stranger down by the lake.
Then I could wear a ball gown made of foam
or drink too many scorch-lengths of gin
or be any old squirrel I see scampering across the grass
—but then wouldn't I be crazy
for the black walnut with its inscrutable shell,
for the juice of the hull that holds the meat, that stains the
    sidewalk, the patio,
that leaves the stucco of the house pockmarked with kisses
and is impossible just impossible to wash out?

# WHY I SING

Night! you klepto surgeon,
wish I could ransack your pockets
for my good days back. Like the summer
I spotted a dead seal tossed up on the beach
and mistook it for a yard of black silk
that I could wind around my neck and wear
to a party—so maybe the boys would notice
my eyes glittering like cracked glass
the exact color of the sea. I was beautiful then
in my confusion. I'm not sure how
this was any different from transforming
some cups of water into wine,
then grabbing the mic to get things started.
So what if we all just want to be cut
loose? So what if we all want to make out
shapes among the clouds? Let's keep at it
for as long as there's a sky
to steal, someone to get broken and glued.

# DAUGHTERS

who pocket lipstick from checkout lines,
who crayon their names on your wall,
who seesaw between seasons
and are seeds the wind plants
on the craggy backs of bears, who claw
their way out of your body
with jewels of blood bedecking their hair,
who click click click across the coliseum
of the Internet in their strappy silver heels, who wander
idle roads of summer and climb into the fretwork
of their guitars, who mark the moon as a jaw
breaker which they will lick down
to its sweet bonewhite heart,
who wear their mothers' breasts
out 'til they're two skinny dogs tied up in a yard,
who fetch you cottonwood fluff, who estrange you
from the loneliness you cherished
and string together a broken necklace
worth of your years, who winter, who are wheat
pennies turned up in dirt, who bury
their faces in sheets and veils, who wait
at the mall for boys to buy them Slurpees
as little pink iPhones vibrate
in the pillows of their hands, who call you
names, who sometimes kiss you, who slant
rhymes for no reason, and need none.

# HOLDING IT UP TO THE LIGHT

My children went to war
on the shore of Lake Superior
over a brilliant green bead of beach glass
recycled from what was once
a Rolling Rock bottle.
Enough, I said,
grabbed it from both their hands, and
threw it into the cold
water, our mother who steals
and bestows. Later
my daughter strung the ones
that looked most like ice (beautiful
zeros she called them) into a necklace
and then gazed at herself in the mirror
as if into that original inland sea.

## ON BEING ASKED BY MY DAUGHTER
## IF I CAN CRY UNDERWATER

Of course I can, because I love to feel
useful. In fact, my tears are quite instrumental
& sound like Brahms handing out penny candy
to children. Salt water taffy! Licorice wheels!
It's like the rain is two days late plus I forgot
my ticket, so I'm running into the sadness
of August & hamsters, whatever the stars
pedal around in that furious orchestra
they set up in the sky. Let us reach, my darling
engine, the speed of a circus cage swimming
with light, an armada of squids opening
like jeweled umbrellas among the weeds.
Here comes the rain & all its etceteras—
the drumrolls, the windows weeping.
Now it's really coming down.

# LOVE IN THE LONG MARRIAGE

You know how it is

impossible to create
seasons. The open seed

catalogue sells us

just a bluster
of might. As spring is

a promise and its future

rot: a glut of crabapples
in August over-

sugaring the air.

# RECKONING

Because the river is always
somersaulting into tomorrow
and isn't singing

*Hosanna* or *Forgive me*
but something more

like *Commit yourself*
*to the open mouth of the sea.*
There everything is washed-

up or spit back or
swallowed, as if nothing can be

gotten or forgotten for good.
The sea worries it's just a bathtub,
agitates against the cold rim

of the sky, while someone in the dark
works out numbers at a desk

as if x really equals why
we are here. Flip to the back
of the book. No answer but *See:*

*whales.* So hard to believe
they're not beautiful balloons of air,

no, I mean plum blossoms,
O God I mean
mirrors and licorice and sheen.

# POEM IN THE SHAPE OF A WINDOW OR A BRICK

As a child, I heard the world end
when my neighbors smashed glass
bottles in the alley, which happened
often. To invent out of the open
window of a feverish sleeplessness
—anthem, dream, or certain bright
apocalypse—that's the beauty we are
given to bear. Who knows how
we visit, or are visited. How many
hands it takes to build the temple, or
hammer numbers over every door.

# A SMALL HYMN

Whatever's woven in bright
looms of grass or looped

in the wheelhead of a seed:
thank you for that.

And for the mineral blueprints
of bone. Also for hooves in the blood

and for whatever choirs, or cries out,
or sleeps in the riverbed

while water runs on, unlistening.
For whatever gets left

at the secret altars night builds
in every closed flower, and that I

(even in my smallness,
thankfully) will never get to see.

# NOTES

"Clogged / only with / Music, like / the Wheels of / Birds," wrote Emily Dickinson on an envelope scrap. My poem with this title was written in response to Billy Collins's "Taking Off Emily Dickinson's Clothes."

A line from "Instructions on How to Play the Comb" is borrowed from Walt Whitman's "Song of Myself," in which the grass is "the beautiful uncut hair of graves."

"Have Torn Off the Whole of May" includes variations on two phrases from Virginia Woolf's *The Waves*: "I have torn off the whole of May and June...and twenty days of July" and "it is tempting now and then to go blackberrying."

A *faena* (from "Dear Professor") is a series of passes and maneuvers a matador makes right before he kills the bull.

The moment in pregnancy when a mother first begins to notice fetal movements is referred to as the "quickening."

In "Beautiful Pathology," the line "Oh! The acceleration with which my heart does proceed" is borrowed from "Poem" by Denis Johnson.

"Casida of the Weeping" is also the title of a poem by Federico García Lorca.

"A Small Hymn" owes thanks to Dean Young's "Spring Reign."

# ACKNOWLEDGMENTS

Grateful acknowledgment to the editors of the publications where the following poems first appeared, at times in earlier forms:

*Anti—:* "Duet" and "Choreography of One Winter" (the latter as "Remainder")

*Black Lawrence Press Blog*: "The Greatest Show" (as "Little Dream Gumball Machine")

*Bridge Eight*: "Nobody"

*Cider Press Review*: "The Clearing" (as "Variations")

*Cream City Review*: "Clogged Only with Music Like the Wheels of Birds" (as "Betrothed—Without the Swoon")

*DIAGRAM*: "An Open Letter To My Imaginary Friend" and "Poem in the Shape of a Window or a Brick" (the latter as "In the Kingdom")

*Hayden's Ferry Review*: "Why I Sing"

*Harpur Palate*: "Transmission" (as "Surround Sound")

*Hobart*: "A Preamble to an Explanation of You" and "Instructions on How to Open a Gift That May or May Not Be a Sausage"

*inter|rupture*: "All That You Have"

*Mead: The Magazine of Literature and Libations*: "Reckoning" (as "Solve For—")

*Paper Darts*: "Flare" and "Instructions on How to Play the Comb"

*Pebble Lake Review*: "Casida of the Weeping"

*Pleiades*: "Dear Professor"

*Poetry City, USA*: "The Universe"

*Revolver*: "Jeopardy," and "Beautiful Pathology"

*Tinderbox Poetry Journal*: "The Quickening," "Jugs," and "On Being Asked by My Daughter If I Can Cry Underwater"

*Tupelo Quarterly*: "Waiting at the Edge of the River Again"
*Whiskey Island*: "Ritual"

"Casida of the Weeping" was selected for the *Best of the Net Anthology 2012* by Sundress Publication.

"A Small Hymn" (originally titled "Thank You Whoever") appeared in *Follow the Thread*, an anthology edited by Alan Cohen.

For their friendship and wisdom, I would like to thank Brett Elizabeth Jenkins, Jay Leeming, Susan Pagani, Kara Olson, Laura McCullough, and Timothy Liu.

Love and gratitude to Tim and Nancy Rauk, Tamara Kaiser, Erik Storlie, and Jeanne Cipar.

Thanks beyond measure to Molly Sutton Kiefer, who kept seeing a book.

Everything (and beyond) for my loves—Adam, Freya, and Oliver.

Katharine Rauk is the author of the chapbook *Basil* (Black Lawrence Press) and has poems published in *Pleiades, Harvard Review, DIAGRAM, Tupelo Quarterly, Best of the Net 2012*, and other journals. She lives in Minneapolis and teaches at North Hennepin Community College.